WOULD YOU RATHER

RATHER

BOOK FOR KIDS

TRY NOT TO LAUGH CHALLENGE

BY UNCLE BOB

Illustrations by Steve Harlan
Cover designed by Angie Gerard

CONTENTS

RULES OF THE GAME

The rules are very basic.

- First of all, you need at least two players and you have to decide who is 'Player A' and 'Player B.' If you have a large group, you can even play with teams.

- Sit across from each other and make eye contact.

- We have 10 rounds and starting with 'Player A', read the question aloud and pick an answer. The same player will then explain why he/she chose that answer in the most hilarious way possible. Don't forget to use your silliest faces to get your opponent to crack a smile.

- If the reason makes 'Player B' laugh or even crack a smile, then 'Player A' gets a point.

- Take turns going back and forth, then mark your total laugh scores at the end of each round.

- Whoever gets the most laugh scores is officially crowned the 'Lord of the Laughs'!

REMEMBER, IF YOU ARE LAUGHING, YOU ARE LOSING!

Let's Get Cracking!

ROUND 1

"Funny & Silly Questions!"

WOULD YOU RATHER...

Have a belly button on
your forehead

~OR~

A nose on your belly?

Never be able to
bend your elbows again

~OR~

Straighten your
knees again?

Laugh Score ___/2

WOULD YOU RATHER...

Have two blue tongues dragging on the ground

~OR~

Three purple noses on the back of your head?

Be able to jump from cloud to cloud

~OR~

Ride the lightning like a horse?

Laugh Score ⬚ /2

WOULD YOU RATHER...

Change your face color
depending on your mood

-OR-

Have your nose growing
whenever you lie?

Wear your underwear
on your head every day

-OR-

Wear shoes on your hands while
walking barefoot?

Laugh Score ⌐__/2

6

WOULD YOU RATHER...

**Be shaken
in a snow globe**

 ~OR~

**Live in a sandcastle that is constantly
changing its shape?**

**Be a giant
with tiny hands**

 ~OR~

**A dwarf
with a huge head?**

Laugh Score ⌷___/2

7

WOULD YOU RATHER...

Have elastic arms that can reach the other end of the earth

~OR~

Have springs on your feet that can help you skip the buildings?

Have your favorite toy come to life

~OR~

Get ten new toys you've always wanted?

Laugh Score ___/2

WOULD YOU RATHER...

Always have roller skates glued to your feet

~OR~

A fan attached to your head?

Have hedgehog spines for your hair

~OR~

A colorful snail shell on your back?

Laugh Score ____/2

9

WOULD YOU RATHER...

Be a huge walking eye

-OR-

A huge sniffing nose?

Be able to create
your own future

-OR-

Change any event
from the past?

Laugh Score ___/2

10

Player B

WOULD YOU RATHER...

Have a neck two feet long that can't stand up straight

~OR~

Not have it at all?

Have your tongue get stuck to an icicle

~OR~

Your fingers super glued to each other?

Laugh Score ___/2

11

WOULD YOU RATHER...

Have a robot that does everything for you

A robot that doesn't stop telling jokes?

Be a fly chased by a fly swatter

An ant chased by an antbear?

Laugh Score ____ /2

12

WOULD YOU RATHER...

Eat with a numb hand

Walk with a numb leg?

Have a beard
that reaches the floor

A mustache that you can wrap
around your head?

Laugh Score _____ /2

Add up your points
and record them below!

Player _____ **/ 20**
ROUND TOTAL

Player _____ **/ 20**
ROUND TOTAL

Round 1
Winner _____

ROUND 2

"Outta This World Questions!"

WOULD YOU RATHER...

fall asleep
next to a vampire

~OR~

Walk beside a zombie?

Make a potion that will turn your
enemy into a pig

~OR~

Utter spells that will turn your
enemy into a plush doll?

Laugh Score ___/2

WOULD YOU RATHER...

Be a pirate who is scared
of the sea and ships

~OR~

A dragon who is scared
of knights and fire?

Find E.T. in the garage

~OR~

Meet Casper at
the haunted house?

Laugh Score ____/2

WOULD YOU RATHER...

**Be able to
see through walls**

~OR~

Hear sounds miles away?

**Set a chimney trap
for santa claus**

~OR~

**A mouse trap under the pillow
for the tooth fairy?**

Laugh Score ___/2

(Player B)

WOULD YOU RATHER...

Be turned into
scarecrow on a farm

~OR~

Into a snowman
on a mountain?

Kiss a frog that will turn
into a prince

~OR~

A pig that will turn
into a princess?

Laugh Score ____/2

WOULD YOU RATHER...

Mumble like minions so nobody
can understand you

-OR-

Make annoying sounds
like Scooby-Doo?

Be lost in a maze with a parrot
that doesn't stop talking

-OR-

Trapped in a vicious forest with
a bunch of angry rabbits?

Laugh Score ⊂___/2

20

WOULD YOU RATHER...

Be the clumsy helper of
santa claus in the toy factory

~OR~

Get stuck in a chimney while helping
him bring gifts to the children?

Step on a sea urchin with
your bare feet

~OR~

Hug a cactus?

Laugh Score ___/2

(Player A)

WOULD YOU RATHER...

fall into a black hole that can't
stop spinning

~OR~

Swallow a bell that doesn't
stop ringing?

Be a superhero
with a silly costume

~OR~

A wizard with a cape made
from a towel?

Laugh Score ⌐___/2

22

Player B

WOULD YOU RATHER...

Be spider-man who can't remember how to shoot sticky webs

~OR~

Batman who forgot how to fly?

Meet an alien whose weapon is a stinky fart

~OR~

A forest monster whose weapon is bad breath?

Laugh Score ___/2

(Player A)

WOULD YOU RATHER...

Have ears that keep growing
as you get older

~OR~

A nose that constantly
shrinks until one day it's gone?

Have zebra stripes all
over your body

~OR~

Be born with
a crocodile jaw?

Laugh Score ____/2

WOULD YOU RATHER...

Not be able to look in the
mirror ever again

~OR~

Get stuck in the mirror
for the rest of your life?

Have spongebob squarepants
as your best friend

~OR~

Plankton as your enemy who tries to
steal your recipe every day?

Laugh Score _____/2

25

Add up your points
and record them below!

Player ____ **/ 20**
ROUND TOTAL

Player ____ **/ 20**
ROUND TOTAL

Round 2
Winner _____

ROUND 3

"Weird Questions!"

WOULD YOU RATHER...

Be a baby
wearing a suit

~OR~

A grown up
wearing a diaper?

Be able to only
walk backwards

~OR~

To only run ahead?

Laugh Score ____/2

WOULD YOU RATHER...

Have a hairy face
for a day

~OR~

Red spots all over your body
for the rest of your life?

Have one purple horn on
your forehead

~OR~

A hairy long tail?

Laugh Score ⎯⎯/2

WOULD YOU RATHER...

Laugh whenever you are sad

~OR~

Sing whenever you are angry?

Live 2 thousand years ago

~OR~

2 thousand years from now?

Laugh Score ⎯⎯/2

30

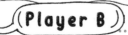

WOULD YOU RATHER...

Sneeze every ten minutes

~OR~

Hiccup whenever you blink?

Have a triangle head

~OR~

A cube–shaped body?

WOULD YOU RATHER...

Wear your grandpa's underwear
to school

~OR~

Your grandma's hairstyle
to the playground?

Speak through
your belly button

~OR~

Burp through your bum?

Laugh Score ___/2

(Player B)

WOULD YOU RATHER...

Be a bunny without ears and a tail

~OR~

A chicken without a beak and wings?

Swallow your goldfish

~OR~

Drink water from a fishbowl?

Laugh Score [____/2]

WOULD YOU RATHER...

Own a snail–sized bear

A bear–sized snail?

Have a remote control that will silence your mom's voice

A magic button that will silence your dad's snoring?

Laugh Score ___/2

34

WOULD YOU RATHER...

Be able to catch a shooting star that will fulfill your wish

-OR-

Touch a rainbow that will turn you into a superhero?

Wrapped in toilet paper all day

-OR-

Have a toilet seat stuck on your head?

Laugh Score ___/2

(Player A)

WOULD YOU RATHER...

Fight a mosquito as a ninja

~OR~

Get rid of a spider with
a karate move?

Have a cake smashed
onto your face

~OR~

Ten chewing gums glued
to your hair?

Laugh Score ⬡__/2

WOULD YOU RATHER...

**Be trapped
in a spinning ball**

~OR~

In a flying balloon?

**Have a huge red pimple
on your nose**

~OR~

**Long hair coming out
of your ears?**

Laugh Score ⬚ /2

Add up your points
and record them below!

Player ____ **/ 20**
ROUND TOTAL

Player ____ **/ 20**
ROUND TOTAL

Round 3
Winner _____

ROUND 4

"Gross Questions!"

Player A

WOULD YOU RATHER...

Lick a sweaty armpit

Someone's dirty foot?

Spill a garbage
can on your head

Wipe your face
with a dirty cloth?

Laugh Score ⟨___/2⟩

40

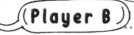

WOULD YOU RATHER...

Wash your hands with stinky cheese soap

~OR~

Wash your hair with fish shampoo?

Fart in front of your whole class

~OR~

Burp in front of your crush?

Laugh Score /2

WOULD YOU RATHER...

Have a house
full of rats

~OR~

A bed full of
worms?

Have a booger hanging from your
nose while singing at a school play

~OR~

Get explosive diarrhea at your
birthday party in front of
all your friends?

Laugh Score ____/2

42

WOULD YOU RATHER...

Drink the juice of vinegar,
mustard, and sugar

~OR~

Eat a cake of oil, egg,
and mayonnaise?

Take a bath in
a squid filled tub

~OR~

Be covered
with 20 leeches?

Laugh Score ⎾___/2⏌

43

WOULD YOU RATHER...

Eat fish food

Lick a live squid?

Have frodo's hairy feet

Kiss gollum's bald head?

Laugh Score ___/2

WOULD YOU RATHER...

Put your finger in your
grandpa's nostril

-OR-

Kiss your grandma's
dentures (false teeth)?

Eat from a plate
licked by a pig

-OR-

Share the same
spoon with a cow?

Laugh Score [/2]

WOULD YOU RATHER...

**Wear a wet
mop on your head**

~OR~

**Rub your back
with a toilet brush?**

**Use a straw that fell into
someone's puke**

~OR~

**Drink water from the glass in which
your grandma holds her false teeth?**

Laugh Score ⌐__/2

WOULD YOU RATHER...

Sniff dog's poop

-OR-

Touch a dirty diaper?

Have a booger fight
with your friends

-OR-

Be hit by fluid
from someone's pimple?

Laugh Score ⬭ /2

47

WOULD YOU RATHER...

**Wear an onion necklace
around your neck**

~OR~

**Carry a dead fish
on your head all day?**

Drink a jar of sweat

~OR~

**Eat a bowl of
someone's boogers?**

Laugh Score _____/2

WOULD YOU RATHER...

Let the wasp sting you on the tongue

~OR~

A worm enter your nose?

Have a transplanted goat head on your body

~OR~

A pig head?

Laugh Score ⎯/2

Add up your points
and record them below!

Player ___ **/ 20**
ROUND TOTAL

Player ___ **/ 20**
ROUND TOTAL

Round 4
Winner ___

ROUND 5

"Animal
Questions!"

WOULD YOU RATHER...

Get a pig with
chicken legs

-OR-

A cow with
an elephant trunk?

Let a crab
grab your nose

-OR-

Let a kangaroo
knock you out?

Laugh Score ___/2

(Player B)

WOULD YOU RATHER...

Have a talking dog
with two heads

-OR-

A flying cat
with three tails?

Let your wet dog jump
on your bed

-OR-

Have your dog fart whenever
it sits next to you?

Laugh Score ___/2

WOULD YOU RATHER...

Get on a bus
with a sparrow driver

~OR~

A taxi with
a giraffe driver?

Breathe fire
like a dragon

~OR~

Spray water
like an elephant?

Laugh Score ____/2

WOULD YOU RATHER...

**Be a monkey with
a red bum at the zoo**

-OR-

**Sleeping bear who forgot to
wake up at the end of winter?**

**Have a cat as
lazy as garfield**

-OR-

**A dog as
loyal as snoopy?**

Laugh Score ⬚/2

WOULD YOU RATHER...

Start each sentence with
a quack like a duck

~OR~

End each sentence
with a moo like a cow?

Be stinky
like a stinky bug

~OR~

Fat like a hippo?

Laugh Score /2

WOULD YOU RATHER...

Be raised by a bunch
of silly monkeys

~OR~

Be born from an egg
in a chicken coop?

Have a bald bunny for
your best friend

~OR~

A crazy wasp
for your enemy?

Laugh Score ___/2

WOULD YOU RATHER...

Be stuck in an elevator
with a stinky skunk

~OR~

Sleep next to
a slimy giant squid?

Sleep upside down
like a bat

~OR~

Walk funny
like a penguin?

Laugh Score ____/2

58

WOULD YOU RATHER...

Dare to enter a basement
full of snakes

-OR-

An attic
full of spiders?

Be a parrot repeating
the same word

-OR-

A cat trying to
catch its shadow?

Laugh Score /2

WOULD YOU RATHER...

See a monkey
take a bath in your tub

~OR~

A pig to eat
from your plate?

Have talons on your
feet like an eagle

~OR~

Three claws on your hands
like a sloth?

Laugh Score ___/2

WOULD YOU RATHER...

Fly on the
back of a pigeon

~OR~

Dive on the
back of a dolphin?

Have a pet with a horse body
and a duck head

~OR~

A dinosaur body
with a bunny head?

Laugh Score ____/2

61

Add up your points
and record them below!

Player _____ / 20
ROUND TOTAL

Player _____ / 20
ROUND TOTAL

Round 5
Winner _____

ROUND 6

"Travel Questions!"

WOULD YOU RATHER...

Travel in the luggage
storage on a plane

-OR-

In a refrigerated
truck for 5 hours?

Sit on a bus next
to a man farting

-OR-

Next to a man
sweating?

Laugh Score ___/2

(Player B)

WOULD YOU RATHER...

Ride in a car with cube-shaped wheels

~OR~

A bike without pedals?

Sleep in a hostel with ten strangers

~OR~

A hotel with dirty beds?

Laugh Score /2

WOULD YOU RATHER...

Camp with a bear in
front of your tent

~OR~

See a badger stealing
your marshmallows?

Be stuck in a museum with
a boring tour guide

~OR~

Stay locked in the
zoo all night?

Laugh Score ____/2

66

(Player B)

WOULD YOU RATHER...

Have a seasickness
on board

-OR-

A fear of heights
on a plane?

Be stuck on a roller coaster
hanging upside down

-OR-

Down the water slide with
the exit closed?

Laugh Score ⬚/2

67

WOULD YOU RATHER...

Walk naked in antarctica

~OR~

Lie on the beach in a snowsuit?

Ride an elephant in india

~OR~

Run away from a bull in spain?

Laugh Score ___/2

WOULD YOU RATHER...

Have the opportunity to jump with a parachute

~OR~

Experience scuba diving?

Sit on a plane next to a vomiting baby

~OR~

Next to a baby with a stinky diaper?

Laugh Score ____/2

69

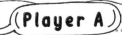

WOULD YOU RATHER...

**Meet tarzan in
the jungle**

-OR-

Dracula in romania?

**Be late to your flight and find
out it was the only one**

-OR-

**Get on the wrong flight and go to the
other end of the world?**

Laugh Score ___/2

70

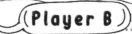

WOULD YOU RATHER...

**Spend all day trapped
in a suticase**

**Carry a backpack
all your life?**

**Travel around the world riding
the slowest turtle**

**Being left alone
on the moon?**

Laugh Score ⟨___/2⟩

WOULD YOU RATHER...

Have your ship captured
by pirates at sea

 ~OR~

Be chased by a wild tribe
on a desert island?

Have all the photos from
your trip be blurry

 ~OR~

Lose all the souvenirs and
gifts you bought?

Laugh Score ____/2

WOULD YOU RATHER...

Have the animals eat all your
camping foods

-OR-

Not be able to light
the fire needed for the grill?

Forget to bring your skis
to the mountain

-OR-

Your swimsuit to
the beach?

Laugh Score ⎧___/2

73

Add up your points and record them below!

Player ___ **/ 20**
ROUND TOTAL

Player ___ **/ 20**
ROUND TOTAL

Round 6 Winner _____

ROUND 7

"food and Drink Questions!"

WOULD YOU RATHER...

Eat pizza that will make you
fart uncontrollably

~OR~

Ice cream that will make
you laugh uncontrollably?

Have a dad with a watermelon
instead of his head

~OR~

A mom with noodles instead
of her hairstyle?

Laugh Score ___/2

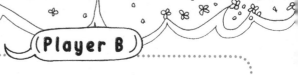

(Player B)

WOULD YOU RATHER...

Eat pepper flavored chocolate

Drink onion juice?

Have a pear–shaped head

A banana nose?

Laugh Score ____/2

WOULD YOU RATHER...

Be friends with
ten coffee beans

Be a mother to
an uncooked egg?

Be covered with honey
in front of a bear

Covered with fruit juice
in front of a hive?

Laugh Score ___/2

(Player B)

WOULD YOU RATHER...

Have a giant roast turkey as your dance partner

-OR-

Play hide and seek with a tiny gingerbread man?

Wear an onion–smelling shirt

-OR-

Pour cold juice into your underwear?

Laugh Score [___]/2

WOULD YOU RATHER...

Not be able to eat ice cream on the hottest day of summer

~OR~

Not be able to drink hot chocolate on the coldest day of winter?

Brush your teeth with mustard

~OR~

Wash your hair with mayonnaise?

Laugh Score ___/2

WOULD YOU RATHER...

Graze grass like a cow

~OR~

Eat bamboo like a panda?

Pour salt into grandma's tea

~OR~

Sugar into grandpa's soup?

Laugh Score [____/2]

81

WOULD YOU RATHER...

**Run away from giant meatballs
rolling down the hill**

~OR~

**Be stuck between
two burger buns?**

**Have an egg fight with
the easter bunny**

~OR~

**A battle of halloween treats
with live pumpkins?**

Laugh Score ____/2

WOULD YOU RATHER...

Give a helmet to a mouse to
avoid the cheese trap

-OR-

A knife to a fish to get rid
of a fishing net?

Sleep on a bed of
strawberry pudding

-OR-

Take a bath in a tub filled
with chocolate milk?

Laugh Score ⬚ /2

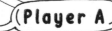

WOULD YOU RATHER...

Eat a jar of pickles

-OR-

Drink a bottle
of vinegar?

Own a chocolate factory where
naughty monkeys run the machines

-OR-

A candy factory where workers
are lazy sloths?

Laugh Score ⬭/2

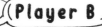

(Player B)

WOULD YOU RATHER...

Sing holding a cob of corn
instead of microphone

-OR-

Play pumpkins
instead of drums?

Go to school with smudged ketchup
all over your face

-OR-

To the birthday of your crush
with green food leftovers between
your teeth?

Laugh Score ⌐___/2

85

Add up your points
and record them below!

Player _____ **/ 20**
ROUND TOTAL

Player _____ **/ 20**
ROUND TOTAL

Round 7
Winner _____

ROUND 8

"Family
Questions!"

WOULD YOU RATHER...

Have a mischievous brother
like dennis the menace

~OR~

An annoying sister
like dee dee?

Have your family members
dressed in a bunny costume
for a family portrait

~OR~

Dressed as elves for
a christmas card?

Laugh Score ⎝___/2

WOULD YOU RATHER...

Have ten younger sisters that
you have to babysit

~OR~

Ten older brothers that
you have to listen to?

Replace your body with
your grandmother

~OR~

Your brain with your
100-year-old grandfather?

Laugh Score ⬚/2

89

WOULD YOU RATHER...

Dare to break your mom's
favorite vase

To make the scratch
on your dad's car?

Let your mom carry you like a baby
in front of your friends

Let your dad sit next to you
on your date?

Laugh Score ____/2

WOULD YOU RATHER...

**Have maggie simpson
as your sister**

-OR-

**Stewie griffin
as your brother?**

**See your grandpa wearing
makeup and a bathrobe**

-OR-

**See your grandma shaving
her head and dancing?**

Laugh Score [____]/2

91

WOULD YOU RATHER...

Travel with your large family
in a small car

~OR~

Be locked in your house alone
for ten days?

Have your mom moo
like a cow

~OR~

Your dad bark
like a dog?

Laugh Score /2

WOULD YOU RATHER...

Live with the adams family in a haunted house

-OR-

With the flinstones family in a cave?

Find out that your mom has a hidden superpower

-OR-

That your dad is a secret agent?

Laugh Score ___/2

93

WOULD YOU RATHER...

Have all your family members
with Mr. Bean's face

~OR~

Have all your family members wear
the same clothes all the time?

---

find out that your grandfather
is a vampire hunter

~OR~

That your grandmother
is a dragon mother?

Laugh Score [___/2]

Player B)

WOULD YOU RATHER...

Have your baby brother bite
you on the finger

-OR-

Have your baby sister pull
you by the nose?

Have all your family members
speak a foreign language you
don't understand

-OR-

None of your family members
recognize you?

Laugh Score ____/2

5

WOULD YOU RATHER...

Be stuck in the 'get along' shirt with your sister

-OR-

Have to walk in the 'get along' pants with your brother?

Wear the clothes of your sibling of the opposite gender for one day

-OR-

Wear identical clothes as your sibling for the rest of your life?

Laugh Score ____/2

WOULD YOU RATHER...

Trade your mom
for a popcorn machine

-OR-

Your dad for
a candy dispenser?

Have your grandmother
with a mustache

-OR-

Your grandfather wearing your
grandmother's skirt?

Laugh Score _____ /2

97

Add up your points
and record them below!

Player _____ **/ 20**
ROUND TOTAL

Player _____ **/ 20**
ROUND TOTAL

Round 8
Winner _____

ROUND 9

"School Questions!"

(Player A)

WOULD YOU RATHER...

**Wear a tutu
on the playground**

~OR~

Pajamas at school?

**Give a presentation in front
of your class naked**

~OR~

**Give a presentation farting
uncontrollably?**

Laugh Score ___/2

100

(Player B)

WOULD YOU RATHER...

forget to write during
the school test

-OR-

Mumble like a baby when a teacher
tells you to read a poem in front
of your class?

Have a globe–shaped head

-OR-

Ruler-shaped legs?

Laugh Score ____/2

101

WOULD YOU RATHER...

Carry your fat friend on
your back all day

Call your teacher a mom in front
of your whole class?

See your teacher with
a tail hidden under her skirt

Your school principal with horns
hidden under his hat?

Laugh Score ___/2

102

Player B

WOULD YOU RATHER...

Be a clumsy wizard at
hogwarts school

~OR~

A mutant at x–mansion unable to
control his powers?

Realize that all your school
friends are aliens

~OR~

All your teachers
are robots?

Laugh Score ⬡ /2

WOULD YOU RATHER...

Have your science teacher turn into a monkey

~OR~

Have your physical education teacher turn into a fat hippo?

Play football wearing a pink dress

~OR~

Come to a dance class wearing a jersey?

Laugh Score ⬭___/2

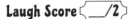

WOULD YOU RATHER...

Bring a pig in a skirt on a leash to school

-OR-

Sit next to a brainy possum with big reading glasses?

Enter the school wearing mismatched shoes

-OR-

Wearing pink fuzzy slippers?

Laugh Score ___/2

WOULD YOU RATHER...

Have a stuttering friend who needs eternity to say one sentence

-OR-

A friend who can't stop talking?

Find yourself in a diaper, sucking your thumb in the school hallway

-OR-

Find yourself on the playground wearing only a towel and clown wig?

Laugh Score ⌐___/2

WOULD YOU RATHER...

Show up at school riding a super fast broom

Fly on a talking magic carpet?

Have your shorts torn while doing squats

-OR-

Fart while doing crunches in psyhical education?

Laugh Score ⬚/2

107

(Player A)

WOULD YOU RATHER...

Have a red lipstick scribbled
all over your face

-OR-

A cat's bum on your forehead drawn
by your friend while you were
sleeping during a boring class?

Be hit by a wet sponge and turn into
spongebob squarepants

-OR-

Be hit by a book and turn
into brainy smurf?

Laugh Score ___/2

108

(Player B)

WOULD YOU RATHER...

Enter the classroom walking
on your hands

~OR~

Crawling on all
fours like a baby?

Get in a school bus with
a stinky sweaty driver

~OR~

A bus full of chickens
and geese?

Laugh Score _____/2

Add up your points
and record them below!

Player _____ **/ 20**
ROUND TOTAL

Player _____ **/ 20**
ROUND TOTAL

Round 9
Winner _____

ROUND 10

"Place Questions!"

WOULD YOU RATHER...

Sleep in an igloo with ten penguins having a tea party

~OR~

In a teepee with a fat grumpy buffalo?

Live with your ten annoying clones in your next life

~OR~

Chase your crush with the mace in your past life?

Laugh Score ____/2

112

WOULD YOU RATHER...

Live in alaska and kiss by rubbing your nose like eskimos do

~OR~

Live in japan and bow when you meet someone not knowing when to stop?

Have a world tour with your rock band made of donkeys

~OR~

Have a dance performance with cheerful monkeys?

Laugh Score ___/2

WOULD YOU RATHER...

Swim on
a snowy beach

-OR-

Ski down
a muddy mountain?

**Be the captain of a flying ship with
a crew of silly dancing pirates**

-OR-

**A pilot on a wingless plane with
thick sweaty stewards?**

Laugh Score ____/2

114

WOULD YOU RATHER...

Have a meteor pull you through space uncontrollably

-OR-

Fall into a black hole that would turn you into an amoeba?

Live on mars with aliens farting through their mouths

-OR-

On saturn with aliens burping through their bums?

Laugh Score ⬚/2

115

WOULD YOU RATHER...

Share your juice with an alien you found in area 51

~OR~

Share your sandwich with the loch ness monster?

Live your whole life in a submarine with poultry

~OR~

In a space capsule with a talking parrot?

Laugh Score ____/2

WOULD YOU RATHER...

Fly around the world, launched out of a cannon

-OR-

Have your feet glued to the ground so you can't go anywhere?

Live in a hive with a grumpy queen

-OR-

In an anthill with a demanding ant boss?

Laugh Score ___ /2

117

WOULD YOU RATHER...

Juggle ten eggs riding
a unicycle in a circus

-OR-

Have a naughty monkey steal
your chips at the zoo?

Live in a house where everything
is upside down

-OR-

In a house where everything
is duplicated?

Laugh Score ⎦__/2

WOULD YOU RATHER...

Be king kong eating a croissant
at the top of the eiffel tower

~OR~

Be godzilla showering
at niagara falls?

Be able to straighten
the leaning tower of pisa

~OR~

Bring to life the great sphinx
of giza with your kiss?

Laugh Score [____/2]

(Player A)

WOULD YOU RATHER...

Be able to hop into
a giant soap bubble

~OR~

fly on an origami dragon?

Live in a house made
of colorful legos

~OR~

Drive a car that can transform
into a transformer?

Laugh Score ___/2

(Player A)

WOULD YOU RATHER...

Eat pizza while surfing

-OR-

Drink soda while skiing?

Cross the entire great wall of china by riding the slowest turtle

-OR-

Climb mount everest on the back of the most clumsiest mountain goat?

Laugh Score ____/2

121

Add up your points
and record them below!

Player _____ **/ 20**
ROUND TOTAL

Player _____ **/ 20**
ROUND TOTAL

Round 10
Winner _____

CONCLUSION

Finally, before you go, I'd like to say "thank you" for purchasing my book and I hope that you and your kids had as much fun reading it as I had writing it.

I know you could have picked from dozens of books on the Would You Rather Game book, but you took a chance with my book. So, big thanks for purchasing this book and reading all the way to the end.

Now, I'd like to ask for a *small* favor. If you and your kid like my book, could you leave a review for this book on Amazon by returning to your order history, the top right-hand side of your screen or the top left-hand side if you're using phone. It will only take a minute to do this.

The book review from you will help me continue to write the kind of books that will help you get results and let other new clients to know more about my book.

I bid you farewell and wishing you and your family a lot of love and happiness!

Thank you and good luck! ☺

— Uncle Bob

ABOUT THE AUTHOR

Robert Ellis, a.k.a Uncle Bob, is the eldest child and only son with three younger sisters of a former school teacher and nurse mother from Boston, Massachusetts. He wasn't always the funniest & smartest kid at school... but one fateful day everything changed for him.

When Uncle Bob was a 10-year-old boy, he received a very old and a super rare book of jokes as a birthday gift from his grandma. It was definitely the best present in his life. Since then, his dream to become a children's book author and to write the most hilarious jokes became an obsession.

Uncle Bob is also a dad of two funny goofy kids and husband of a beautiful wife.

In his spare time, Uncle Bob loves to hike, fish, visit the beach, and do anything remotely adventurous, like zip-lining.

As an author, He hopes to inspire children to have a love of learning and a passion for reading. He is excited to share his work with you!

Hopefully, his books will make people all around the world a little bit kinder, healthier, and happier!

Made in the USA
Coppell, TX
24 November 2020

41738894R00075